Oxford Progressive English Readers
General Editor: D.H. Howe

Stories of Shakespeare's Plays 2

The *Oxford Progressive English Readers* series provides a wide range of reading for learners of English. It includes classics, the favourite stories of young readers, and also modern fiction. The series has five grades: the *Introductory Grade* at a 1400 word level, *Grade 1* at a 2100 word level, *Grade 2* at a 3100 word level, *Grade 3* at a 3700 word level and *Grade 4* which consists of abridged stories. Structural as well as lexical controls are applied at each level.

Wherever possible the mood and style of the original stories have been retained. Where this requires departure from the grading scheme, definitions and notes are given.

All the books in the series are attractively illustrated. Each book also has a short section containing questions and suggested activities for students.

Stories of
Shakespeare's Plays 2
Wyatt & Fullerton

Hong Kong
OXFORD UNIVERSITY PRESS
Oxford Singapore Tokyo

Oxford University Press

Oxford   New York   Toronto
Petaling Jaya   Singapore   Hong Kong   Tokyo
Delhi   Bombay   Calcutta   Madras   Karachi
Nairobi   Dar es Salaam   Cape Town
Melbourne   Auckland

and associated companies in
Berlin   Ibadan

Illustrated by Marion Bird
Cover illustration by Tomaz Mok
Simplified according to the language grading scheme
especially compiled by D.H. Howe

First published 1973
Thirteenth impression 1990

ISBN 0 19 638232 7

Printed in Hong Kong by Skiva Printing & Binding Co., Ltd.
Published by Oxford University Press, Warwick House, Hong Kong

Contents

1 The Merchant of Venice

When the city of Venice in Italy was rich and famous, one of her chief citizens was a merchant named Antonio. Antonio, Merchant of Venice, was a rich man who owned many valuable ships and traded with foreign countries. He was well known for his kindness, and had many friends. Amongst his friends was a young Venetian nobleman called Bassanio. Although he was a noble, Bassanio was poor. He spent more money than he could afford, so as to live in the way he liked. But Antonio loved him, and always lent or gave him money when he needed it.

Bassanio loved a wealthy and noble young lady named Portia, whose father had recently died. Portia was not only wealthy, she was beautiful and clever too. Princes and noblemen were continually asking to marry her. These men were able to show their wealth and rank by arriving at her house with expensive presents and many servants. Bassanio could not afford to buy expensive presents. He was afraid Portia would not consider marrying him because he was so much poorer than all the others.

Bassanio went to his great friend Antonio to see if he could help him. He told Antonio that Portia seemed to like him. Bassanio thought that if only he could go to visit her like a rich nobleman, he might be successful. If Antonio would lend him enough money, Portia might agree to marry him.

'I am always willing to help you, Bassanio,' said Antonio, 'but I have no money to spare just now. All my ships are at sea. However, I shall have plenty of money when they come back. Until then, I shall borrow some for you, from Shylock.'

Shylock the Jew was a well-known money-lender in Venice. He had become very wealthy, but he still loved making more

money, and he hated spending it. He was not popular in the city because he was so mean. People who could not pay back the money they owed him got no mercy from Shylock. Antonio had often made clear to other people that he had no
5 respect for Shylock because of the way he treated those in debt to him. Antonio himself had many times lent money without asking for any profit, and this spoilt Shylock's business. For these two reasons, Shylock hated Antonio, and was waiting secretly for an opportunity to harm him.

10 Bassanio went with his friend Antonio to borrow 3,000 ducats* from Shylock. 'I shall be able to pay it back as soon as my ships come to port. As you know, they are now at sea and will soon arrive home with valuable cargoes,' said Antonio to Shylock. 'I never lend money for profit, or borrow money
15 either, but because Bassanio is my great friend, I will do it for him.'

At first Shylock seemed unwilling to lend the money. He knew well what Antonio had said about the way he lived. 'Your ships may be destroyed by storms before they reach
20 Venice,' he said, 'and then you will be unable to pay me the money.'

Then he decided to offer Antonio a bargain. 'I am willing to be friends with you, and I will lend you this money for no profit. This will show you that I too can be kind and generous,
25 in spite of what you have said about me. But I have had an amusing idea, and I hope you will agree to it. If you do not pay me in time, I shall cut a pound of your flesh from any part of your body I choose.'

Bassanio was suspicious of Shylock's intentions, and told
30 Antonio not to accept this plan. But Antonio laughed, and agreed to the joke, and the three men went to a lawyer to sign the agreement. Antonio then took the money from Shylock and gave it to Bassanio, who prepared to visit Belmont where Portia lived.

*ducat, a piece of gold money.

The three boxes

Portia's father had been very anxious that she should choose the right husband. So before he died he invented a plan to help her to do this. He had three small boxes made of different metals. The first box was made of gold, the second box of silver and the third box of lead.* One of these boxes contained a picture of Portia. Her father wished her to marry the first man to guess which box contained the picture. Each man must make a promise: if he guessed wrong, he would never ask any woman to marry him. Portia felt she must be obedient to her father, even now, after his death. She feared that a man she did not like would find the picture, but still she intended to do what her father had asked.

When they heard about this plan, many men did not dare to guess at all, and went away. This was a great relief to Portia, for she had not liked any of her visitors yet. She told her servant, Nerissa, that they were dull, or had no sense of humour, or were cross. One of the men who did dare to choose was a prince from Morocco. He had chosen the gold box. He thought that only a gold box was good enough for Portia's picture. When he opened it he found only a terrible picture of death inside. The next man to guess was the Prince of Aragon, in Spain. He chose the silver box. On the box were these words: 'The man who chooses this box will get what he deserves.' This seemed fair, thought the prince. If he was not fit to marry Portia then he should not be allowed to. But surely he deserved her! The prince was very hopeful when he opened the box. Inside was not a beautiful picture of Portia, but a picture of a mad fool. He too went away disappointed.

Then Portia heard that Bassanio had arrived. He had brought with him a friend called Gratiano. Gratiano was in love with Nerissa, Portia's servant. He hoped to persuade Nerissa to marry him while Bassanio was asking Portia to be his wife.

*lead, a heavy grey metal, dull to look at and much less valuable than gold.

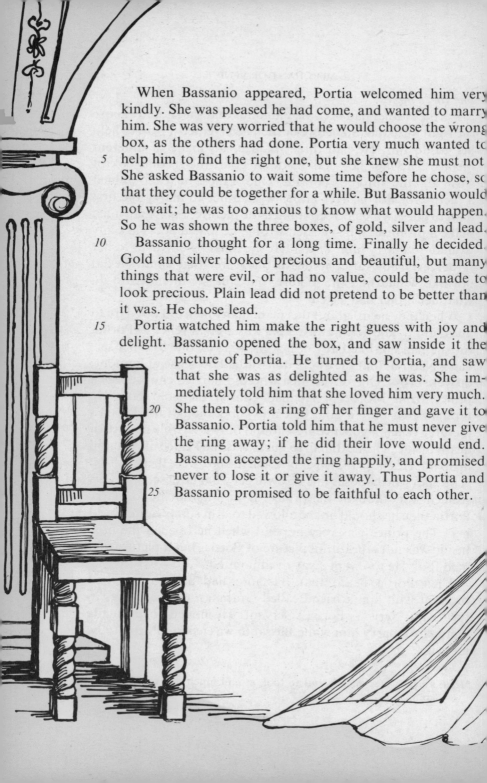

When Bassanio appeared, Portia welcomed him very kindly. She was pleased he had come, and wanted to marry him. She was very worried that he would choose the wrong box, as the others had done. Portia very much wanted to
5 help him to find the right one, but she knew she must not. She asked Bassanio to wait some time before he chose, so that they could be together for a while. But Bassanio would not wait; he was too anxious to know what would happen. So he was shown the three boxes, of gold, silver and lead.
10 Bassanio thought for a long time. Finally he decided. Gold and silver looked precious and beautiful, but many things that were evil, or had no value, could be made to look precious. Plain lead did not pretend to be better than it was. He chose lead.
15 Portia watched him make the right guess with joy and delight. Bassanio opened the box, and saw inside it the picture of Portia. He turned to Portia, and saw that she was as delighted as he was. She immediately told him that she loved him very much.
20 She then took a ring off her finger and gave it to Bassanio. Portia told him that he must never give the ring away; if he did their love would end. Bassanio accepted the ring happily, and promised never to lose it or give it away. Thus Portia and
25 Bassanio promised to be faithful to each other.

Antonio in trouble

Gratiano and Nerissa were in the room at the same time, and had seen everything. Gratiano now came forward and said he hoped Portia and Bassanio would be very happy. He said that he and Nerissa would like to be married at the same time.
5 Portia and Bassanio were very pleased, and agreed at once.

But then something happened which worried them all a great deal. A messenger arrived with a letter for Bassanio from his friend, the merchant Antonio. Bassanio read the letter, and his face became pale. The letter contained very bad news.
10 Portia quickly asked what had happened. And now, for the first time, Bassanio told her about the money he had borrowed. He told her too about Antonio's arrangement with Shylock. This letter showed that Antonio's ships had not come back to port; they had been wrecked at sea, and all his cargoes
15 had been lost. His ships were lost, and now he would have to give Shylock a pound of his flesh. Antonio had been unable to pay back the money, and the date for him to do this had already passed. 'I am now certain to die, and want to see you,' he wrote.
20 The messenger told them that Shylock had continually asked the Duke* of Venice to deal with the matter. He wanted to be paid his pound of flesh immediately. And so poor Antonio was in prison, waiting for his trial.

When Portia heard this terrible story she wanted to help
25 in any way she could. She offered to pay Shylock much more than the 3,000 ducats he was owed. She told Bassanio to go and help his friend as soon as possible. However, Portia insisted on one thing: they must be married before Bassanio left Belmont. So all four of them went at once to the church
30 and were married. Bassanio and Gratiano then left their wives and went straight back to Venice.

Portia thought a great deal about the problem. She wanted to save Antonio's life, because he had been so generous to her husband Bassanio. Finally she sent a letter to a cousin of hers,

---

*Duke, a nobleman of high rank, often the ruler of a small State.

who was a well-known and clever lawyer. She asked him for
his advice, and she also asked him to lend her his lawyer's
clothes. Her cousin, Dr. Bellario, immediately sent her the
clothes and told her how Antonio should be defended.

Portia had decided what she would do. She told her friends   5
and servants that she was going away for a few quiet days
until her husband returned. Then she called Nerissa and
informed her of the plan. They dressed themselves in men's
clothes and set off for Venice.

Meanwhile Bassanio and Gratiano had arrived in Venice,   10
where the trial would soon begin, under the direction of the
Duke of Venice. Antonio and Shylock were brought before
the Duke. He asked Shylock to give up his cruel demand, and
not to take a pound of Antonio's flesh. But Shylock would not
agree. Then Bassanio offered to pay him twice as much money   15
as he was owed. Still Shylock would not let Antonio go. 'The
laws of Venice allow me to demand a pound of Antonio's
flesh, because he has broken our agreement. I hate Antonio,
and I will not be persuaded. I would rather have Antonio's
flesh than any money I am offered.'   20

Turning to the Duke, Shylock said, 'Will you permit me to
do what I have a right to do, or have you no respect for the
laws of Venice?'

The young lawyer

The Duke had to admit that the law did allow Shylock to
refuse the money instead of Antonio's flesh. He did not dare   25
to treat Antonio differently from any other citizen. If Shylock
insisted, Antonio would have to die. Shylock did insist. He
thought to himself, 'At last I shall be able to treat Antonio in
the way he deserves. I do not pity him. This proud merchant
always hated me and made others hate me too. I will not   30
forgive him.'

The Duke had sent for a lawyer to advise him about this
difficult problem. The man to whom he had written was Dr.
Bellario—the man who had given his advice and his lawyer's
clothes to Portia. As Shylock would not show any mercy, the   35

Duke decided to wait for the lawyer. 'Perhaps this clever lawyer can find a way to save Antonio's life,' he thought.

Just as he had decided this, a clerk came in. He said he had brought a letter from Dr. Bellario. In this letter the lawyer
5 wrote that he was ill, and would not be able to come to the trial. However, he asked if a young friend of his could come instead. The Duke gave his permission, and invited the young lawyer to come in.

The clerk who brought the letter for the Duke was really
10 Nerissa, dressed as a man. The young lawyer was really Portia, dressed in Dr. Bellario's clothes. The Duke was surprised when he saw how young the lawyer was, but he asked him to defend Antonio.

Portia turned to Shylock and asked him to show mercy to
15 Antonio. 'Mercy,' she said, 'rewards not only the man who receives it, but also the man who gives it. We pray to God, hoping he will show us mercy, and we should show mercy to other people.' But Shylock would not listen to her.

'I only ask to be paid what I am owed,' he said.
20 'Can he pay back the money you lent him?' asked Portia.

Bassanio quickly said, 'He can pay it, and he is willing to pay more. I can pay ten times as much for Antonio.' Bassanio prayed to the lawyer to forget about the exact words of the law, in order to save a life.
25 'No,' said Portia, 'I cannot do that. If we do not insist that this man obeys the law now, others may follow his bad example, and the country will suffer.'

Shylock was delighted when he heard this answer. 'Oh wise young judge!' he cried, excited. He expected the trial to
30 end very soon. He praised the lawyer and laughed at Antonio. Portia then asked to see the agreement Antonio and Shylock had signed. She read it, and agreed that Shylock could claim his pound of flesh. Then Portia turned to Antonio and commanded him to bare his chest. Shylock was ready to kill
35 Antonio. He called out, 'Oh noble judge! Oh excellent young man!'

Antonio also thought he was going to die. He said good-

bye to his friend Bassanio; he asked him to tell Portia why he
had died. Bassanio was very unhappy, and he replied that he
would give anything he had to save Antonio if he could. He
would give his own life, or even his wife, to help Antonio.

'Now,' said Portia to Shylock, 'take the pound of flesh that   5
is owed to you. Cut it from this man's chest.'

Shylock had his knife in his hand as he moved forward. He
was ready to cut out Antonio's heart. 'Oh wise judge! Oh
wise judge!' he cried. To Antonio he cried, 'Prepare yourself!'

Shylock is defeated

But before he could strike Antonio with his knife, Portia   10
stopped him.

'Wait!' she said. 'I have something else to say. By this agreement you are not allowed to take one drop of blood. The words
say clearly, "a pound of flesh". This flesh you may take, but
if you spill one drop of blood then all your property must be   15
given to the State. That is the law of Venice.'

Shylock stood completely still. He was so surprised and
annoyed he could hardly speak. 'Is that what the law commands?' he asked. Portia offered to show him the law on the
subject. Gratiano could see how angry Shylock was, and now   20
he cried out, 'Oh wise judge! See, Shylock, he is a wise judge!'

Shylock then remembered that Bassanio had offered to pay
back the money, and even to pay him more. 'I will accept your
offer,' he said to Bassanio. 'Pay back three times as much as
I lent Antonio, and then I will let him go.'   25

'Here it is,' said Bassanio, holding out the money. But Portia
would not allow this. A little while ago Shylock had refused
the money, so now he should have nothing.

Shylock, very angry, was about to leave when Portia called
him back. 'Wait!' she said. 'There is another law we must   30
remember. If a non-Venetian plans to kill a Venetian citizen,
half his property is given to that citizen. The other half is given
to the State. And the Duke may order any other punishment
he thinks is fit. Kneel in front of him and pray for mercy.'

Shylock had so recently refused mercy to Antonio that he   35

could not now expect mercy for himself. But the Christian
Duke was not so cruel as the Jewish money-lender.

'I will show you that men can be much kinder to each other
than you think. You will not lose your life; I will tell you this
even before you ask me to save you. But you must give half
your money and property to Antonio, and half to the State.'

And now the good Merchant of Venice showed mercy to the
money-lender. 'I will not take my share of Shylock's wealth.
But he must become a Christian.'

Shylock was also forced to sign a will. This will said that
Jessica, his daughter, and Lorenzo, her husband, should receive all Shylock's money when he died. Lorenzo was a good
friend of Antonio's. Not long before this, Jessica had run
away from her father and married Lorenzo, a Christian, secretly. She had taken some money and jewels with her when
she left home, and Shylock had been very angry. At first he
could only shout, 'My daughter! Oh my ducats! Oh my daughter! She has run away with a Christian! The law! My ducats
and my daughter!' Shylock seemed to be just as worried about
his money as he was about his daughter. The money-lender
had said then that he would not leave Jessica any money when
he died, and he would never forgive her.

The Jew now knew that he must obey Portia's and Antonio's
commands. 'I am ill,' he cried. 'Let me go home. Send the will
to my house. I will sign it.'

So the Duke let Shylock go, and the trial ended.

During the trial everyone had been very surprised to see how
young and wise the lawyer was. But no one had suspected that
the lawyer was really Portia. Even Bassanio had not guessed.
Portia had changed her appearance and voice so cleverly that
he could not recognize her.

Portia's trick

Bassanio and Antonio wanted to show the lawyer that they
were very grateful for his help. 'Please accept the 3,000 ducats
owed to Shylock,' Antonio said. But Portia would not accept
the money. Bassanio was also very anxious to give the lawyer

something. So Portia thought she would trick her husband, for a joke. 'If you insist, give me your gloves,' she told Bassanio. Bassanio took off his gloves, showing the ring on his hand. 'As a sign of your love, give me that ring on your finger.' Bassanio immediately drew his hand away. This ring was the *5* one Portia had given him when she promised to marry him, and he had promised never to give it away. He pretended the ring had no value, and was too small to give as a present. But Portia asked for it again. Bassanio then told her it was his wife's ring, and she had made him promise never to give it *10* away.

'That is a common excuse,' replied Portia. 'That is what men say when they do not want to give a present. Your wife will not be angry with you for long. You can tell her how much I deserved the ring.' *15*

Portia and Nerissa, still dressed as a lawyer and a clerk, turned to go. Almost immediately Antonio persuaded Bassanio to give up the ring. Bassanio felt ashamed to seem ungrateful, and gave it to Portia. Nerissa also cleverly managed to persuade Gratiano to give her the ring she had given to him. *20* He too had promised never to give it away.

Portia and Nerissa left Venice, and went as quickly as possible to Belmont. They wanted to get there before their husbands returned. When they got back to Portia's house, they changed their clothes at once. Soon they were sitting down, *25* dressed in their ordinary clothes, waiting for their husbands to return. Not long after, the two men arrived, with Antonio. Bassanio introduced Antonio to his wife. 'This is the friend,' he told her, 'who has helped me so much.' Portia welcomed Antonio to her house. *30*

While she was doing this, she saw Gratiano and Nerissa quarrelling in a corner of the room. 'What is happening?' cried Portia. 'Are you quarrelling already? What is the matter?'

'We are arguing about a ring which Nerissa gave me,' *35* Gratiano explained. 'The ring had these words written on it: "Love me and never leave me".'

'I am annoyed because Gratiano promised faithfully that he would keep it, and now he has given it away to a lawyer's clerk. It does not matter whether it was a valuable ring or not. He should not have given it away.'

A happy ending

5   Portia was now determined to enjoy the trick she had played on her husband. 'Of course Gratiano was wrong to give away his wife's first present. I, too, gave my husband a ring, and made him promise to keep it. If he gave that ring away, I would be very angry with him indeed.'

10   Then Gratiano replied, 'But Bassanio did give his ring away —he gave it to the lawyer who asked for it. And then the boy, his clerk, asked me for my ring.'

When she heard this, Portia pretended to be very angry. She asked Bassanio, 'Which ring did you give him? I hope it 15 was not the ring you accepted from me.'

Bassanio felt very unhappy when he saw how angry his wife was. But he had to admit that he had given the ring away. 'I wish you knew how unwilling I was to give the ring away, and to whom I gave it, and why I gave it to him.'

20   But Portia still pretended to be angry. She accused him of giving the ring to a woman. Bassanio thought Portia must think he was very unkind. He told her he had given the lawyer the ring because he was so grateful to him for saving Antonio's life. 'If you had been there,' he said, 'I think you would have 25 told me to give him the ring.'

Then Antonio turned to Portia and said, 'These unhappy quarrels have all been caused by me!'

'Do not treat this matter so seriously,' replied Portia. She took the ring from her bag and said, 'Give him this ring, and 30 tell him to keep it better than he kept the last one.'

Antonio passed the ring to Bassanio, who looked at it. He was surprised to see that it was the one he had given away. Portia then showed her husband the letter from Dr. Bellario, and so he discovered that the clever lawyer was really Portia, 35 his wife. Bassanio realized that his own wife's courage and

wisdom had saved the life of his dear friend Antonio. He was
surprised and delighted.

Soon afterwards Antonio received good news about his
own affairs. Portia handed him some letters which had just
arrived. These told Antonio that the ships which he thought   5
were lost had returned to Venice. They had brought back
valuable cargoes. Antonio was a wealthy man again.

Thus the strange story of the Merchant of Venice ended—
with good news for the merchant, and with laughter between
the husbands and wives over the joke about the rings.   10

2 Macbeth

Macbeth was a great Scottish nobleman who commanded the army of Duncan, King of Scotland. He was the Thane* of Glamis, and belonged to the same family as the King. War broke out between Duncan and some of his noblemen who refused to obey him as their ruler. They were helped by the King of Norway, who landed in Scotland with an army to fight King Duncan. Macbeth and Banquo, two of the King's faithful generals, had been sent to attack the disobedient nobles.

After a terrible fight, King Duncan's men defeated their enemies, and the King of Norway was forced to ask for peace. In the battle, Macbeth fought with great bravery; all the soldiers and messengers talked about him and praised his conduct. Duncan, the King, wanted to reward him by giving him a new honour. The Thane of Cawdor had fought with the King's enemies and had been captured. Duncan decided to make Macbeth the new Thane of Cawdor.

The two generals were returning from the battle across a wild and lonely piece of country. Suddenly three evil-looking old women appeared in front of them. These old women were witches.* Macbeth was frightened by this awful sight, and he asked the witches who they were. The answer he received from the first witch was, 'Welcome, Macbeth! Welcome, Thane of Glamis!' The second witch cried, 'Welcome, Macbeth! Welcome, Thane of Cawdor!' The third witch cried, 'Welcome, Macbeth! You will be King!'

*Thane, a nobleman in early England; this title does not now exist.
*witch, a strange woman who has the power to use magic, and who has knowledge that ordinary humans do not have; her power is often thought to come from the devil, and she ususally uses it for evil purposes.

Macbeth was so shocked by this that he could not speak. The witches then turned to Banquo and spoke to him. 'You are less important than Macbeth, and yet more important. You will not be so happy, and yet you will be happier. Your children will be Kings, though you will not.' Macbeth de-   5
manded an explanation from the witches, but he had spoken too late: they had disappeared as quickly as they had come.

As Macbeth and Banquo stood discussing these strange words, two nobles sent by Duncan rode up to them to praise the generals' victory. They told Macbeth that the King wished   10
to reward him, and had therefore made him Thane of Cawdor. Macbeth could not believe what he heard. But when he was sure it was true, he began to think about the other promise the witches had made. Could he really become King of Scotland? Banquo remained calmer, and warned Macbeth not to trust   15
the witches too much. He realized that Macbeth was allowing himself to think dangerous and wild thoughts. But Macbeth could not stop thinking about what the witches had said. He wondered what he could do to make their words come true. He was shocked by the ideas he had. Perhaps, after all, if it was   20
his fortune to be King there would be no need for him to do anything.

After Macbeth's victory, Duncan told him that he would like to honour him with a visit to his castle. When Macbeth heard this, he asked to be allowed to go home at once to pre-   25
pare for the royal visit. Before he set off he sent a private letter to his wife, Lady Macbeth. In this letter he told her that he had met the witches, and what they had said. He also told her that some of the witches' words had already come true. He encouraged his wife to believe that she might one day be Queen of   30
Scotland. From this day on, Macbeth could think of nothing else. When Duncan announced that his elder son, Malcolm, would be King after him, Macbeth wondered how he would manage to deal with this difficulty.

Lady Macbeth

When Lady Macbeth read her husband's letter she was   35

determined that he should rule Scotland. She was sure that
Macbeth would have to act without mercy for others. He
would have to make himself King, but she was afraid he was
too kind to do it. Lady Macbeth knew her husband would love
5   to be King, but she realized that she would have to urge him to
do it. She decided that Duncan must be murdered while he was
staying with them at their castle that night. Lady Macbeth did
not believe anyone would discover who had done the murder.
She was certain that Macbeth was so well loved and admired
10 that no one would think that he had killed the King. As soon
as Macbeth came home, she told him about her plan. She
advised him to show no sign that anything was wrong, and to
welcome his guests cheerfully. She ended her orders with the
words, 'Leave all the rest to me.'

15   The King arrived, and was welcomed by Lady Macbeth
with great respect. Duncan was pleased. The castle garden
seemed calm and beautiful after the battle, and it was very
pleasant to rest and to be amongst friends. Here he thought he
could forget, for a while, the troubles of his kingdom. He had
20 supper with Macbeth, who showed him the room where he
would sleep. When the King went to bed he felt peaceful and
happy. He was so pleased with the kindness of his host and
hostess that he sent a wonderful diamond to Lady Macbeth as
a present.

25   But Macbeth felt neither calm nor peaceful. He was sure he
could not do this murder, and there were many good reasons
why he should not do it. He could not kill one of his own rela-
tives, in his own castle. He was responsible for Duncan's safe-
ty because the King was his guest. Besides, he was such a good
30 and fair King that it seemed particularly wicked to kill him.

While Macbeth was considering what to do, Lady Macbeth
came into the room. He told her he could not kill Duncan.
'The King has given me great honours already, and I am very
popular with the people. I am grateful for this; it is enough for
35 me.' His wife told him that she would never respect him again,
and that she would always think of him as a useless coward.
She told him that they would certainly succeed if they were

determined enough. She explained to him how easy it would be
to murder Duncan without anyone finding out. Macbeth
changed his mind, and agreed to do everything his wife suggested. They put medicine in the wine of the two guards who
slept in Duncan's room to make them sleep. Then Macbeth   5
would be able to murder Duncan while he slept.

When all her guests had gone to bed and the castle was
quiet, Lady Macbeth crept along to the King's room. Duncan
and the two servants were sleeping. She held a knife in her
hand, and she meant to kill Duncan. However, when Lady   10
Macbeth saw him lying there peacefully in the moonlight, he
reminded her of her dead father and she could not do it. She
returned to her husband. She gave him the knife and
commanded him to go and do the deed.

Murder of a King

Macbeth crept through the darkness, with the knife in his   15
hand. As he went, he saw a terrible sight. A knife, covered in
blood, appeared before his eyes. The handle was turned towards his hand. He put out his arm to reach the knife, but it
was not real. Macbeth went on towards Duncan's room, but
he was now even more frightened than before.   20

As Macbeth moved back towards the door after killing
Duncan, he heard one of the servants laugh in his sleep. The
other servant cried 'Murder!' as he dreamt. Both awoke, but
they did not see Macbeth, and they went to sleep again. In her
room Lady Macbeth waited very anxiously for her husband to   25
return. She listened to every sound, and when she heard the
servants moving in the King's room she thought Macbeth had
failed. At that moment he came back, and told her he had done
the murder.

But Macbeth's peace and happiness had been destroyed for   30
ever by the crime. He was very shocked, and dared not think
about what he had done. He thought he could hear a voice
crying, 'Sleep no more; Macbeth shall sleep no more.' His
wife scolded him for his weakness, and for bringing the knife
back from Duncan's room. It was covered in blood. She told   35

him to go back and put it beside the King's servants, and to put some of Duncan's blood on them. But Macbeth did not dare to go back and see what he had done, so Lady Macbeth went instead.

5 Macbeth could not rest. His mind was full of wild thoughts and fears, and every noise frightened him. He kept on staring at his hands, which were covered with blood. He imagined that they would never be clean again, and would make everything he touched red with blood. Lady Macbeth returned. Her
10 hands were now covered with blood, but she told her husband, 'A little water will clear away this deed. How easy it is then!' She commanded him to go to bed as if nothing had happened. People would be suspicious if they were discovered awake and dressed in the middle of the night.

15 The weather that night was wild and stormy. Early in the morning there was a loud knocking sound. Two of Duncan's noblemen, Macduff and Lennox, had come to offer their services to the King. A little while after their arrival, the murder was discovered. Soon everyone had heard the dreadful news.
20 Duncan's two sons, Malcolm and Donalbain, were staying at the castle too. As soon as Macbeth was told of the murder, he went out and killed the King's two servants as they slept, with their own knives. He hoped in this way to hide his own guilt.

Malcolm and Donalbain, after a short and urgent discus-
25 sion, decided to escape abroad. They did not think that their lives were safe. The person who had killed Duncan in order to be King would surely try to kill his sons, because they ought to succeed him. One went to England, the other to Ireland, and some men were certain they had escaped quickly because they
30 were guilty of the crime. Macbeth was then the nearest relative to Duncan left in Scotland, and so he became King at once. The words of the witches had come true.

Banquo's ghost

However, Macbeth did not feel safe now that he was King. After his terrible crime he could not trust others. He was par-
35 ticularly afraid of Banquo, who had been with him when the

witches spoke to him. Banquo knew that Macbeth had been excited by the witches' words, and that he really wanted to be King. Besides, the witches had said that the kingdom would one day be ruled by Banquo's family. This thought made Macbeth both angry and afraid. He had risked his life when he 5 murdered Duncan. He wondered whether he had helped Banquo even more than himself. Macbeth felt that he could not safely allow him to live, and he decided to murder his son also. Because he was frightened and because he was deter- mined not to lose the kingdom he had just won, Macbeth 10 planned to murder again.

In order to kill Banquo, the new King and Queen gave a great feast for the chief nobles. They invited Banquo and his son, Fleance, as the most important guests. That day, Banquo and Fleance went out riding but, before they got back to the 15 castle, they were attacked by three men. Macbeth had paid these men to kill Banquo and Fleance but, in the struggle, Fleance escaped. Though Banquo had been murdered his son managed to get to England, and his family did later become Kings of Scotland. In spite of all Macbeth's plans, the things 20 the witches said to Banquo came true.

The time for the feast arrived, and the King and Queen sat down with their guests. The Queen welcomed everyone, and was determined to delight her guests. Macbeth talked freely with the nobles, and everyone was pleased with the feast. 25 Macbeth said cheerfully that he hoped his two chief guests would soon arrive. Suddenly he rose from his seat, trembling with fear. All the visitors noticed, and wondered what had happened. Macbeth thought he could see the dead Banquo, sitting in the chair that had been kept for him. No one else 30 could see anything. Lady Macbeth tried to calm her anxious guests. She assured them that Macbeth was not really ill. Turning to him, she told him fiercely to control his fear before everyone guessed their secret. At that moment Banquo's ghost* seemed to disappear. Macbeth, with more courage 35

*ghost, the body of a dead person which appears before living people: often it looks strange and frightening.

now, sat down again. He drank some wine, and wished all his
visitors, including Banquo, good health. When he said, 'We
miss our dear friend Banquo, and wish that he were here,'
Banquo's ghost appeared again. Macbeth was helpless with
5   fear and could not bear the terrible sight. He cried out in a
loud voice to the ghost to go away.

Everyone got up, wondering whether Macbeth had gone
mad. They could see nothing. The Queen quickly asked her
guests to leave, in case the King said even more suspicious
10 things. She told them that the King's behaviour was not
unusual, and that these fears did not last for long. However,
Lennox and some other nobles did not forget what had
happened, and were suspicious of Macbeth's strange behaviour. Macduff had not even come to the feast because he feared
15 it might be some kind of trap for the King's enemies. Macbeth
was very frightened; some nobles did not trust him, and
Fleance was alive in England. He was prepared to kill anyone
to defend his position. He decided to ask the advice of the
three witches again—they seemed to know about everything
20 that would happen.

The three witches again

Early the next day, therefore, Macbeth went to the lonely
place where he had met the witches. He found them preparing
magic mixtures from parts of animals and plants. They used
these secret mixtures to obtain knowledge of future events.
25 Macbeth asked them to tell him what would happen to him,
and immediately he saw three devils in front of him. The first
was in the form of a head in armour. Macbeth began to speak
to it, but the witches told him to be silent. Then the head slowly
said, 'Macbeth! Macbeth! Macbeth! Watch Macduff! Watch
30 the Thane of Fife!' After this the head disappeared into the
ground.

The second devil appeared to the noise of thunder. It was
in the form of a child covered in blood. It told Macbeth to be
cruel, bold and determined, and to fear no one. There was no
35 one born to a woman in the ordinary way who could harm

him. Macbeth at once thought of the warning he had just received about Macduff. 'I need not fear him then,' he thought. But he decided to kill Macduff anyway, to be quite safe.

Then a third devil appeared: it was a child dressed like a King, with a tree in its hand. It said 'Macbeth shall never be *5* conquered until great Birnam Wood moves towards Dunsinane Hill!' 'That will never happen,' said Macbeth to himself. He was encouraged by these words. He believed all he had heard, and he felt he need never fear his enemies again.

Before Macbeth left the place, he asked the witches whether *10* any of Banquo's children would become Kings of Scotland. This was the one problem that still worried him. The three old women warned him not to ask this, but he insisted. He heard music and, one by one, eight shadows passed by him. They were the shadows of Kings. The last one was Banquo, covered *15* in blood; he turned his head and smiled at Macbeth. Banquo was holding a mirror in his hand in which Macbeth could see still more Kings. These were all children of Banquo, and would rule after Macbeth in Scotland. Macbeth was very shocked, and cried 'This is a terrible sight! Now I see what it means, for *20* Banquo is pointing to the Kings in the mirror to show that they are his children. Will this really happen?' The witches assured him that it would, and then the sound of the music faded away and they disappeared.

As Macbeth was returning from the witches he met one of *25* his nobles. This man told him that Macduff had left his home and family suddenly, and had gone to England to join Malcolm, Duncan's son. Malcolm hoped to gather an army and to defeat Macbeth. Then he could become King of Scotland, as his father had planned. Macbeth was very angry when *30* he heard this news. He attacked Macduff's castle, and savagely killed his wife and all his children.

This deed, and other actions like it, did little to help Macbeth. Many of his nobles and soldiers hated him for his unnecessary cruelty. Some left him and joined his enemies. *35* Those who stayed with him did not respect or admire him any longer. Macbeth himself was always anxious and unhappy,

and his Queen suffered from terrible dreams because of her guilt. Her servants found her walking around the castle in her sleep, talking wildly about the murder. Finally she died, and many people said she had killed herself.

The moving wood

Macbeth tried to gather an army to fight Malcolm, but he had no friends left, and no one wanted to help him. He began to wish he were dead, but he had enough courage left to come out of his castle at Dunsinane and fight a hopeless battle against his enemies.

While Macbeth was preparing for the battle, a messenger came to tell him that he had seen a strange sight. 'As I was watching on the hill for the enemy I looked towards Birnam, and I thought the wood began to move.'

'You are a liar and a slave!' cried the King. Then he added, 'If you are lying, I will hang you from the nearest tree. But if your story is true I do not care if you hang me instead.' He thought to himself, 'Now I begin to doubt the advice of the witches, who spoke the truth, but tricked me all the time. The words of these devils never mean what they seem to mean.'

Then, fully armed, Macbeth went out to meet his enemy. The messenger had not lied. When Malcolm's army was marching through Birnam Wood he ordered each man to cut down a branch and to carry it forward with him as he went. Thus Macbeth would find it much more difficult to estimate the size of the attacking army. The result was that the whole of Birnam Wood seemed to be moving towards Dunsinane.

In spite of his hopeless situation, Macbeth fought fiercely

and with great courage. He remembered that the witches had said that no one born normally could harm him, and this increased his bravery. He killed many of his enemies, although his own army did not support him well.

5 Meanwhile, Macduff, who was leading the first part of Malcolm's army, was determined to fight Macbeth. He wished to kill the King himself, because Macbeth had murdered his family. At last the two men saw each other. Macbeth tried to avoid the fight. But Macduff rushed towards him, and a fierce
10 fight began. Macduff fought savagely, thinking of his dead family, but Macbeth turned confidently to him, and cried that his life was protected against anyone who had been born normally. Macduff replied that he had not been born in the ordinary way, but had been taken from his mother's body
15 before the proper time. For a moment, Macbeth's courage disappeared. 'I will not fight you,' he cried to Macduff.

Macduff laughed. 'Live, then, a prisoner, and see all men laugh at you as a coward!'

Macbeth replied, 'I will never obey young Malcolm, or be
20 cursed by the people. Fight, Macduff!'

After a great struggle, Macduff killed the King, and cut off his head. He presented it to Malcolm, the new King. Everyone was relieved that the reign of the cruel King Macbeth had ended.

3 The Tempest*

There was an island in the sea, a long way from any other land, which had been controlled by the magic power of an evil old witch called Sycorax. There were only two humans living on this island—Prospero, a wise, white-haired old man, and Miranda, his beautiful young daughter. Another creature lived on the island too, but he was so strange and ugly he could hardly be called human. He was the ugliest creature you can imagine, and more like a monkey than a man. This peculiar and savage animal was Caliban, the son of the witch Sycorax. Sycorax had died before Prospero came to the island. The old man had seen Caliban in the woods one day and had taken him home and tried to teach him. However, he found it was impossible to teach him anything, and so he made the animal his slave. Caliban had to do all the hard and unpleasant work for Prospero and Miranda. He complained continually about this, and did as little work as he could.

Prospero and Miranda lived in a hollow rock which they had made into a house. Here the old man kept lots of books which were very precious to him. He studied magic with them, and this magic gave him some power over the island. He used the magic to free many good spirits* who had been captured by Sycorax. Any spirits who refused to obey her evil commands had been caught and kept in trees. Because Prospero had kindly freed them, these spirits loved him and served him gratefully. The chief spirit was called Ariel; he was always ready when his master called him. He was able to fly through the air without anyone seeing him, and could do many other

*tempest, a very bad storm.
*spirit, a fairy.

things that ordinary humans cannot do. For example, he could change himself into different shapes and become a bear or any other animal. Ariel was very cheerful and active; he used to play all sorts of tricks on the stupid Caliban when the creature was lazy and did not obey Prospero's orders.

One day there was a great storm at sea near the island. Miranda and her father were watching from the shore when they saw a ship amongst the high waves. Miranda thought it was certain to sink, and she felt very sorry for the men in it. She asked Prospero to use his magic powers to calm the sea and save the ship if he could. Prospero told her not to be anxious, for the sailors would not be harmed. 'But now,' he added, 'it is time to tell you how you and I came here, twelve years ago, and where we came from. Sit down and listen, for you must be told this story now.' Miranda sat down and listened carefully. Her father had started to talk about this matter several times before, and then stopped, saying, 'Wait; I will not tell you yet.'

Prospero's story

Prospero began his story. 'Twelve years ago I was the noble ruler of Milan, in Italy, and I had wealth and lands and power. But I preferred to study, and I gave the control of state affairs to my brother Antonio. I should not have trusted him. He wanted my rank as well as my power, and planned to kill me. He persuaded Alonso, the King of Naples, to help him. One dark night they seized you and me, and put us in a ship. Then we were taken out to sea, and put in an old boat that was about to break into pieces. They left us to drown. The man who was forced to make the arrangements for Antonio and the King was Gonzalo, a kind man. Gonzalo did everything he could to help us. He put some water and food and clothes in the boat with us. Knowing that I loved my books more than anything else, he put in the most valuable ones he could find in my library.

'The men on that wrecked ship out there are my enemies, who have been brought to this island by a strange chance.

Alonso, King of Naples, arranged for his daughter to marry the Prince of a country far across the sea. He and his nobles are returning in that ship, from the distant land where the marriage has taken place. With the King is my unfaithful brother, Antonio, now the ruler of Milan. Another brother of mine, Sebastian, is there too; so is the King of Naples's son, Ferdinand, and the kind old Gonzalo. I have used my magic to make the storm which is blowing the ship towards this island.'

Prospero told this story to Miranda as they watched the ship in the stormy sea. Although Prospero had made the storm purposely, he did not intend to harm his enemies. In fact, his intention was quite different. He was going to use his magic to make these men feel sorry for their evil deeds; then he would forgive them, and they would no longer be his enemies.

So Prospero called the chief of the good spirits, the faithful Ariel. Ariel had made the storm when Prospero commanded him to, and now he frightened the men on the ship with all kinds of tricks so that they jumped into the sea. Ferdinand, the King of Naples's son, jumped in first, and swam safely to the shore near to Prospero and Miranda. Ariel assured Prospero that all the men were safe; the sailors were asleep on the ship, and the other royal passengers had landed on another part of the island. However, each group thought that all the others had drowned. Ferdinand wept about his father's death, and his father wept about his.

Miranda saw the young Prince walking towards the place where she and her father were sitting, and she was surprised and delighted. Because she had lived for twelve years alone on the island with her father, Miranda had never seen a young man like Ferdinand. She asked her father whether he was a human or a god. And when Ferdinand saw Miranda he believed she must be a goddess. They loved each other at once, and Prospero was pleased to see this, for he had planned that they should marry each other. However, he wished to test the strength of Ferdinand's love for his beautiful daughter first.

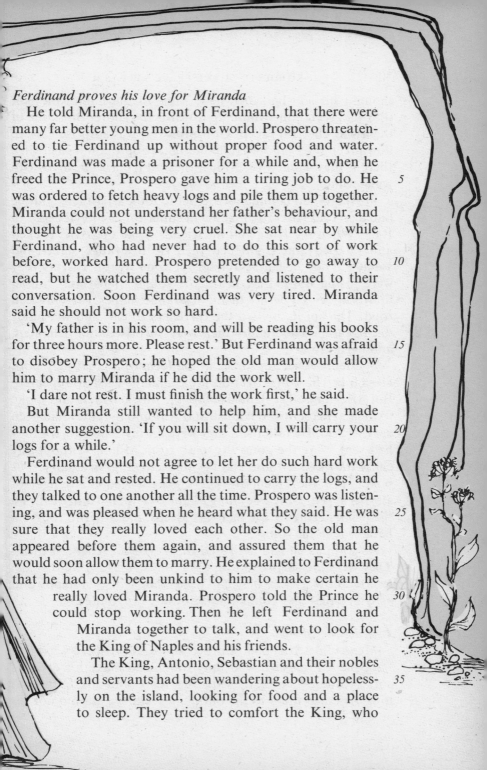

Ferdinand proves his love for Miranda

He told Miranda, in front of Ferdinand, that there were many far better young men in the world. Prospero threatened to tie Ferdinand up without proper food and water. Ferdinand was made a prisoner for a while and, when he freed the Prince, Prospero gave him a tiring job to do. He was ordered to fetch heavy logs and pile them up together. Miranda could not understand her father's behaviour, and thought he was being very cruel. She sat near by while Ferdinand, who had never had to do this sort of work before, worked hard. Prospero pretended to go away to read, but he watched them secretly and listened to their conversation. Soon Ferdinand was very tired. Miranda said he should not work so hard.

'My father is in his room, and will be reading his books for three hours more. Please rest.' But Ferdinand was afraid to disobey Prospero; he hoped the old man would allow him to marry Miranda if he did the work well.

'I dare not rest. I must finish the work first,' he said.

But Miranda still wanted to help him, and she made another suggestion. 'If you will sit down, I will carry your logs for a while.'

Ferdinand would not agree to let her do such hard work while he sat and rested. He continued to carry the logs, and they talked to one another all the time. Prospero was listening, and was pleased when he heard what they said. He was sure that they really loved each other. So the old man appeared before them again, and assured them that he would soon allow them to marry. He explained to Ferdinand that he had only been unkind to him to make certain he really loved Miranda. Prospero told the Prince he could stop working. Then he left Ferdinand and Miranda together to talk, and went to look for the King of Naples and his friends.

The King, Antonio, Sebastian and their nobles and servants had been wandering about hopelessly on the island, looking for food and a place to sleep. They tried to comfort the King, who

5

10

15

20

25

30

35

thought his son had drowned; some of the nobles thought
they had seen him swimming towards the shore. But none of
them was cheerful except Gonzalo, who was surprised to see
how green the island was; he thought people could easily live
5   there if they wanted to. At last they all fell asleep, tired with
wandering.

Prospero had commanded Ariel to look after them; but he
had also told Ariel to make them suffer for their evil deeds in
Italy. When the King and his friends woke up, Ariel tricked
10 and puzzled and frightened them with strange sights and
sounds. They began searching for food again. Just as they
were losing hope, they heard the sound of peculiar music.
Spirits appeared before them, in strange shapes, carrying rich
food. The spirits invited the travellers to eat, and then they
15 disappeared. The hungry men were surprised and delighted,
and began to eat.

Suddenly Ariel appeared, in the form of a great ugly bird.
He clapped his wings over the table, and the feast disappeared.
But Ariel himself remained before the shocked men, and spoke
20 to them. He reminded Alonso and Antonio that they had been
very wicked. He told them they were hardly fit to live, for they
had sent away the good Prospero from Milan. Without any
cause they had left him and his innocent child in a dangerous
boat. Now they themselves had experienced the danger of
25 storms at sea. Only one thing could save them from death on
this island: sorrow for their evil deeds and a desire to live a
better life in the future.

As soon as he had delivered this message, Ariel left them.
They were too surprised to speak. Alonso and Antonio at last
30 realized how wicked they had been; they felt so unhappy and
ashamed that they could not think about anything else.

Leaving the island

Meanwhile Ariel had returned and told Prospero what had
happened. Prospero, who only wanted to make his enemies
sorry, ordered Ariel to send the King and his friends to
35 him. Ariel led them to the old man. Neither Antonio nor his

brother, nor any of the others with them, recognized Prospero, who was dressed in his magic clothes. They had no idea that the man they saw was the former ruler of Milan. Prospero reminded them of the cruel way they had treated him and his daughter in the past. Then he took off his magic clothes, and *5* they saw he was their old ruler. Alonso and Antonio both told Prospero that they were sorry. They promised to give him back his position as ruler of Milan, and prayed to him to forgive them. The old man did forgive them for all their crimes and welcomed them as friends. *10*

The old man then turned to Alonso and said, 'Because you have given me back my kingdom, I will show you something that will give you as much joy.' He stood back, and there, a little way behind him, Alonso saw his son, sitting with Miranda. The father and son were both delighted to see each *15* other alive and well. When he saw Miranda, Alonso, like Ferdinand, thought she must be a goddess.

'No,' replied Ferdinand, smiling at his father. 'She is not a goddess, but human like the rest of us. But the gods have allowed her to be my wife. She is the daughter of the ruler of *20* Milan. After our marriage he will be my father also.'

Alonso replied, 'Then that marriage will make me her father too. So I must ask my daughter to forgive me for my crime against her father.'

But Prospero said they should all forget the past. *25*

That night Prospero gave a feast and Caliban, his slave, served the guests. Everyone was very surprised by the sight of this ugly creature.

The King and his friends wondered how they would be able to get back to Italy. Only Prospero and Miranda knew that the *30* travellers' ship had not been destroyed, and that the sailors had not been drowned. Ariel had done his work well; all the sailors were safe, and the ship was whole. As they were talking at the feast, Gonzalo saw some sailors coming towards them. The men were delighted to see that all their royal passengers *35* were alive, and Prospero's new friends were relieved to hear that the ship was still safe and strong.

'Tonight you must rest here,' said Prospero to his friends, 'and I will amuse you with the interesting story of my life after I left Italy. Tomorrow morning I will show you your ship, and we will set off for Naples. In Naples Ferdinand and Miranda
5   will be married. Afterwards I hope to return to Milan, and to rule there till I die.'

The next day they all left the island. Prospero said good-bye to his faithful spirits, and especially to Ariel. He freed Ariel to go where he liked, but the spirit asked to be allowed to stay
10 with the ship until it arrived in Naples. He wanted to guide it safely home.

Before he left the island, Prospero buried all his magic books, for he had decided never to use his magic powers again. His wishes had all come true—he was friends with his brother
15 again, he would live and rule in Milan again and his daughter would be Queen of Naples. He did not need magic any more.

4 Hamlet

When Hamlet, King of Denmark, died suddenly, his son, the young Prince Hamlet, was very sad. He had loved his father, who was a kind and popular King. His sadness increased greatly when his mother, Queen Gertrude, married again, less than two months after her husband's death. The man she mar-   5
ried was King Hamlet's brother, Claudius. Young Hamlet was very fond of his mother, and was shocked at her behaviour. He knew he would never be able to accept his uncle Claudius as his new father. Claudius had no concern for the feelings of other people; he had no grace, and was ugly to look at. In fact,   10
Hamlet thought, he was not fit to be a King. When the Prince compared his character with the character of his dead father, he could not understand his mother's action. The fact that such a man had control over his mother worried him.

Hamlet was so worried and unhappy that he could not   15
think of anything but his father's death and his mother's re-marriage. He was never cheerful any more; he did not care about how he looked, but wore black clothes, in memory of his father's death, after everyone else had stopped wearing them. He was no longer interested in reading, formerly one of his   20
favourite activities. Everyone noticed Hamlet's sadness, and it annoyed Gertrude and Claudius. It reminded them con-tinually that their son disliked their marriage and still thought about his father, whom they wanted to forget.

The new King and his Queen tried hard to cheer Hamlet   25
up, and asked him not to think about the past, which could not be changed. Their requests had no effect on Hamlet's be-haviour. He thought about the way in which his father had died so suddenly. Claudius reported that the King had been bitten by a snake while he was sleeping in the garden, but   30

Hamlet suspected that this was not true. Often Hamlet wished he were dead, or that he could kill himself, because the future seemed so hopeless.

One day the Prince heard a strange story. The soldiers who
5 guarded the castle at night had seen a ghost. Hamlet's friend Horatio decided to tell him about it, because the ghost looked exactly like the dead King, Prince Hamlet's father. Hamlet questioned the soldiers carefully, and decided that this probably was his father's ghost. If so, it surely wanted to tell him
10 something important. It might even be able to explain how King Hamlet had died. Now that he had heard about the ghost, Hamlet suspected that his father had been murdered.

The next night, therefore, Hamlet, Horatio and one of the soldiers met at midnight to watch for the ghost. It had refused
15 to speak to any of the guards or to Horatio. Everything outside was quiet, but in the distance they could hear the King and Queen drinking and laughing at a feast. Horatio suddenly touched Hamlet on the shoulder.

'Look, my lord,' he whispered, 'look, it comes.' The ghost
20 had appeared again. It was dressed in armour and had a pale face and a silver beard.

Hamlet knew at once that it was his father's ghost, and he was very frightened. 'Why have you left your grave? What does this mean? What should we do? Oh, answer me!' he
25 cried.

But the ghost did not answer. Instead it silently signalled to Hamlet to follow it. Horatio was afraid something terrible would happen to his dear friend, and he prayed to Hamlet not to go. Hamlet fiercely pushed his companions away and
30 disappeared from their sight.

Hamlet's madness

When they were alone the ghost spoke. It told the Prince it was the dead King's ghost; it said that King Hamlet had been cruelly murdered by Claudius. Claudius wanted both to be King, and to marry Gertrude. While King Hamlet was sleep-
35 ing in the garden one day, Claudius had crept up and poured

poison in his ears. When the ghost had told Hamlet how his father died, it commanded him to revenge* this terrible murder. It particularly commanded him, however, not to harm his mother, Gertrude; he should leave her conscience and heaven to deal with her guilt.   5

Hamlet was determined to forget all his own affairs, and all he had planned to do in the future, and to think of nothing but revenge. He would do as the ghost had ordered. When the Prince returned to them he made them promise not to tell anyone what had happened that night. Only his great friend,   10 Horatio, was told the whole story. His companions were worried. They were certain the presence of King Hamlet's ghost meant that something was wrong with the state of Denmark.

Hamlet had been very shocked by this experience, and he was still very frightened. He feared the King and Queen might   15 suspect that he knew how his father had died. This seemed especially likely since they were watching him carefully and were anxious about him already. Hamlet told only Horatio what he planned to do next. He would pretend to be mad so as to hide his real feelings and to appear harmless. Hamlet's   20 talk and behaviour, therefore, became stranger than ever. He seemed to be most mad when he was with the King and Queen, or anyone who was likely to report about him to them. Weeks passed, but Hamlet did not get any better, and the King and Queen could not understand what was the matter with him.   25 They did not think the Prince suspected them, but they did not think that his father's death was enough to make him mad.

Among the nobles of Denmark was Polonius, one of the King's chief ministers. Polonius had a beautiful daughter named Ophelia; before his father's death, Hamlet had told   30 Ophelia that he loved her greatly. She had believed everything he had said to her, and she loved him too. Ophelia had allowed Hamlet to visit her often. However, when her father, Polonius, heard about this, he told Ophelia that she should not be so

---

*revenge, to harm someone purposely, because he has harmed you or
    your family.

willing to see Hamlet. He did not think it was right for a young
girl to show her love for the Prince so clearly. Polonius ordered
his daughter to be less friendly, and Ophelia obeyed him,
trusting his wisdom. She refused to receive Hamlet's letters,
5   and she would not see him.

Soon after, Hamlet came to see her, though he had not been
asked. His behaviour was strange and he seemed frightened
and unhappy. Then he wrote her a letter insisting that he loved
her and would always love her. Polonius rushed to the King
10   to tell him that he had discovered the cause of Hamlet's
madness. He believed Hamlet loved his daughter, and that
her refusal of his love had made Hamlet mad.

By now the King was very worried about the Prince, and
wondered whether he knew about the murder. He decided
15   that Hamlet must be sent away from Denmark and, if possible,
that he must be killed.

The wandering actors

Hamlet's behaviour towards Ophelia was all part of his
plan. He was continually worried by the memory of the ghost,
and what it had ordered him to do. He feared that it might be
20   an evil ghost that had tried to make him murder Claudius, by
telling him lies. And even if it had told him the truth, the murder would not be easy. The Queen was usually with Claudius,
and he was often guarded by soldiers. Most important of all,
Hamlet did not want to do it. He was a thoughtful, serious
25   man who always preferred to think and to study rather than
to act. He could take the decision to kill Claudius but he could
not make himself do it. Hamlet was so worried about what
he had to do that he became even more unhappy and anxious.
'Denmark is a prison,' he told two of the King's nobles, and
30   he added that he could find no reason to go on living. He referred to Claudius and Gertrude as 'my uncle-father and aunt-
mother'.

While Hamlet was in this dreadful state he heard that a
group of wandering actors had come to the castle. Hamlet
35   had seen their plays before, and remembered that one of them

told of the terrible murder of a noble and the sorrow of his wife. Hamlet had an idea. He spoke to one of the actors alone, and asked him if he knew a play called 'The Murder of Gonzago'. In it, a noble called Gonzago is poisoned in his garden by a relative; this relative afterwards marries his widow. The actor said he knew the play, and they would perform it. 'Tomorrow night,' Hamlet said, 'you must act it before the King and Queen, but I want to put in a few lines of my own to improve it.'

So Hamlet made some changes in the play, to make it as like the real murder of his father as possible. He remembered a story about a murderer who had admitted that he was guilty after he saw his crime acted on the stage before him. 'So now,' thought Hamlet, 'when the King and Queen see this play, I will watch their faces very carefully to see what effect it has on them. If they are really guilty of murdering my father they will show it by their behaviour.' Thus he would have definite proof of whether the ghost had spoken the truth or not. And then, he thought, he would know whether to act or not.

Hamlet invited Claudius and Gertrude to see the play, and they accepted the invitation eagerly. They did not know what the play would be about, but they hoped that Hamlet was at last getting better and becoming interested in things again. Hamlet told Horatio what he had arranged, and asked him to watch the King and Queen carefully. In spite of this new plan, Hamlet was still very unhappy and blamed himself for being a coward. He knew he had delayed, and that he should have taken revenge earlier. Once more he thought about killing himself to avoid the terrible deed, but he feared the things that might happen to him after death even more than he feared life.

Hamlet kills Polonius by mistake

When it was time for the play to begin, Claudius and Gertrude entered, and sat down in front of the stage. Hamlet and Horatio sat at one side where they could see the King and Queen well. The play started with Gonzago and his wife talking. She promised faithfully that she would never marry again if her husband died. 'Only those women who have killed the first husband marry a second,' she said. Hamlet saw his mother's face become pale.

5 In the next scene Hamlet eagerly explained the story of the play to the King. 'He is poisoning Gonzago in order to get his lands for himself,' the Prince said. 'The next scene shows how he loves Gonzago's wife.' Claudius was very frightened. He got up suddenly and he and the Queen quickly left the 10 room. Everyone was very surprised, but Hamlet was now certain that Claudius was a murderer. His duty was clear to him.

As Hamlet discussed what had happened with Horatio, a messenger told him that the Queen wished to see him im- 15 mediately. Claudius had suggested that Gertrude should speak to her son to try to discover whether he knew about their se- cret, and why he was mad. Gertrude agreed, and she also agreed that old Polonius should hide in her room behind a curtain to listen to Hamlet too.

20 The Prince was excited by his discovery, and even felt able to do the murder when he went to see his mother. He decided to do as the ghost had ordered; 'I will speak cruelly to her, but I will not do anything cruel.' On his way to Gertrude's room Hamlet saw Claudius, alone, kneeling down to pray. He could 25 have killed him then without difficulty. He was sure that the King was a murderer. Yet Hamlet did not do it. He thought cruelly, 'If I kill him now, while he is praying, he will go to heaven. I would rather kill him when he is angry or has been drinking.' He put away his sword and quietly left the room.

30 As soon as he saw his mother he spoke fiercely to her. 'Now, mother, what's the matter?'

'Hamlet, you have shocked your father very much,' the Queen replied.

'No, mother, you have shocked my father very much,' Ham- 35 let said angrily. She referred to the present King, but Hamlet spoke about the dead King.

'That is a stupid answer,' said Gertrude.

'It was the answer you deserved,' said Hamlet.

The Queen asked him if he had forgotten that she was his mother. Hamlet immediately replied that he wished he could forget it. He was determined to speak to her now that they were alone. He would try to persuade her to end her wicked life. Roughly he took hold of her wrists and forced her to sit down. Gertrude was frightened, and cried out, 'What are you going to do? Are you going to murder me? Help! Help!'

Polonius heard her cries, but could see nothing from where he was hiding. He thought Hamlet must be going to kill his mother, and he called out, 'Help! Help! Help!'

Hamlet immediately raised his sword and rushed to the curtains, realizing that someone was hiding there. He killed the man with his sword and dragged the body out into the room. He was surprised and disappointed when he saw he had killed Polonius—Hamlet thought he had killed the King.

'You have done a cruel and foolish thing!' cried the Queen.

Hamlet answered, 'A cruel thing; almost as bad, mother, as killing a King and marrying his brother!'

The King's plan

Hamlet was now so angry that he blamed his mother for everything, and said all the things that he had wanted to say for so long. He accused Gertrude of forgetting King Hamlet's great love for her. He compared her new husband with the kind, gentle character of the old King. He showed her two pictures, one of each brother; the difference between them was plain. The Queen was shocked and ashamed by Hamlet's dreadful speech and behaviour, and prayed to him to stop, but he would not.

Then suddenly Hamlet stopped speaking, and his face became pale. His father's ghost had appeared again. He stared at the ghost, and spoke to it, and looked frightened. The Queen was sure he was mad again because she could see nothing. The ghost told Hamlet to leave his mother now and say no more. She was weak with sorrow and shame. It reminded him that he had not yet killed the murderer, and urged him not to delay.

Then the ghost left them alone again.

'I must be cruel to you in order to be kind,' Hamlet told his mother, to explain his behaviour. Before he left her, Hamlet asked Gertrude not to live with Claudius as his Queen any more. He asked her to refuse all love to the man who had murdered his father and stolen the kingdom.

By now the King was determined to kill Hamlet, for he realized that the Prince was dangerous. He decided to send him abroad. Polonius's death gave him a very good excuse to do this. He would tell everyone that Hamlet must go abroad to prevent Polonius's family from taking revenge on him. Claudius arranged to send Hamlet to England; he pretended to the Prince that he was being sent there to deal with state affairs. The King planned to send two nobles with him on the journey, and they would carry a letter commanding that Hamlet should be killed as soon as he landed in England.

However, Hamlet knew the King feared him and was an evil man. He suspected Claudius. He sailed from Denmark as the

King had arranged, but he looked for, and found, the letter. Hamlet read it, and then rubbed out his own name and in its place he put the names of his two companions. The letter now seemed to say that these two men should be killed. The
5 Prince closed it and put it back where he had found it.

The next day the ship was attacked by sea robbers. Hamlet acted very bravely. He jumped on to the robbers' ship and fought them alone, while his own ship escaped. He was left with the robbers, who could have killed him. But they admired
10 his courage and, when they found out that he was a Prince, they respected him. The robbers treated him with mercy, hoping to be rewarded for their kindness. They sailed towards Denmark and let Hamlet land at the first port they came to.

Hamlet returns to find Ophelia dead

As soon as he landed, Hamlet wrote a letter to his uncle,
15 telling him that he was in Denmark again. He told the King he would explain everything when they met again the next day. He did not mention that he had discovered the letter. Meanwhile he sent a letter to his great friend, Horatio, telling him what had happened, and asking him to come as quickly as
20 possible. When they met, Hamlet told Horatio that the King had tried to kill him.

As they were going home, they saw a strange sight. Two workmen were digging a new grave for a woman who had just died. Hamlet and Horatio stopped and talked to the men, who
25 were cheerful and joking, in spite of the work they were doing. As they talked together, men and women began to arrive for the funeral.

Hamlet and his friend became very curious when they saw, among the people, the King and Queen. There were other
30 nobles too, including Laertes, Ophelia's brother. They hid themselves and watched as the priest conducted the funeral service. The priest would not give the woman a complete service because, he said, she had probably killed herself. Laertes stepped forward and cursed the priest, crying that his sister
35 would go to heaven. Hamlet suddenly realized that his dear

Ophelia lay in the grave. He could hardly speak, his sorrow was so great.

He saw the Queen scatter flowers on the grave; he heard her say that she had hoped Ophelia would be Hamlet's wife. He heard Laertes, full of sadness and anger, shout out; he saw him leap into the grave. And suddenly Hamlet could control himself no longer. He rushed forward, and jumped into the grave beside Laertes.

'I loved Ophelia! Forty thousand brothers could not love her more! If you will be buried alive with her, so will I.'

Ophelia had been made unhappy by her lover's strange behaviour. When she heard that Hamlet had killed her father she became mad and then drowned herself. Laertes thought Hamlet was responsible for his sister's death as well as for his father's, and he tried to fight with him in the grave. Laertes and Hamlet had to be forced away from each other. The funeral ended and the people went away.

The King was still determined to kill his nephew. He realized that he could use Laertes's anger and sorrow for his own purposes. He had told Laertes that Hamlet killed his father, and he encouraged him to revenge his death. The King suggested that they should arrange a friendly sword fight between Laertes and Hamlet. Laertes would use a sword with a sharp point, although this was not allowed in friendly matches. They would also put poison on the sword so that, as soon as Laertes struck Hamlet, he would be killed. To make quite certain that Hamlet would die, the King would have two bowls of wine near him on the table, and one would contain poison. The King would wish Hamlet success in the match by drinking from one bowl and he would give the other one to Hamlet to drink. Hamlet would be sure to die, either by the poisoned sword or from the poisoned wine.

The truth is known

Hamlet was pleased when he heard about the match. He was eager to test his skill in a friendly fight against Laertes. He had been practising, and thought he had improved his skill. The

Queen and all the nobles gathered to watch the fight. Before it began, Hamlet asked Laertes to forgive him, and they shook hands. At first Hamlet seemed to be fighting more skilfully. When they stopped to rest, Claudius urged Hamlet to take a
5 drink of wine, but the Prince said he would not drink until he had finished the match. Soon Laertes began to fight better, and the match became very exciting. The King was watching the two men so carefully that he took no notice of the Queen who was sitting beside him. She was thirsty, and picked up a
10 bowl of wine to drink. Claudius did not see that she was drinking from the poisoned bowl. At that moment Laertes cut Hamlet with his sharp sword. At once Hamlet seized the sword and wounded Laertes with it. He now knew that Laertes had cheated by using a pointed sword. Hamlet did not know, how-
15 ever, that it was also poisoned, and that they would both die. The Queen fell to the floor, crying 'The drink! The drink! Oh, my dear Hamlet! The drink! The drink! I have been poisoned.' She died almost immediately.

   Hamlet realized that there had been some evil plan, and he
20 saw that he had enemies all round him. He ordered the servants to shut all the doors so that no one could escape. Laertes fell to the floor, but he managed to tell Hamlet what had happened and who was responsible. 'The King! The King's to blame,' he said. He told Hamlet he would not live for more
25 than half an hour. Hearing this, Hamlet rushed to Claudius, holding the bowl of poisoned wine. He forced it down the King's throat, crying, 'Follow my mother!' He had at last revenged his father's death, only minutes before he too would die. Hamlet and Laertes forgave each other for the harm each
30 man had done, and Laertes died.

   Then Hamlet, hardly able to breathe, called his faithful Horatio to his side and asked him to tell the world the true story of King Hamlet's murder and its revenge. Horatio wanted to drink the rest of the poisoned wine, and to die with
35 the Prince. But Hamlet made him promise that he would not, and Horatio lived to tell everyone that Hamlet was an innocent man who would have been a good King.

5 King Lear

Many hundreds of years ago, King Lear was the King of Britain. He had three daughters. Goneril, the eldest, was married to the Duke of Albany; Regan, the second daughter, was married to the Duke of Cornwall; Cordelia, the youngest, had not yet married. King Lear was over eighty years old, and had reigned for a long time. He was tired, and wanted to have time to prepare himself for death. He decided he would give up the control of state affairs and spend the rest of his life in peace and quiet. He loved his three daughters, so he planned to divide his kingdom into three parts and to give one part to each daughter. King Lear had been a noble and respected King, but now that he was old he sometimes had rather strange ideas, and was not a very good judge of other people. He called his three children to him to find out which one loved him best, so that he could give each child the share of the kingdom she deserved.

Goneril was invited to speak first. 'I love you more than I can say in words, more than my life and freedom. I love you as much as any child has ever loved her father,' said Goneril. The King was delighted to hear these words; Goneril had said just what he wanted to hear. Pointing to a map in front of him, he drew a line round one-third of his kingdom and made her the ruler of it.

The second daughter, Regan, was then called. She saw that Goneril's speech had pleased her father, and wanted to please him more than her sister. So she pretended that her love was even greater. 'I love you quite as much as Goneril does,' she said, 'and even more; for I am only happy when I am loving you.' Lear thought he was very lucky to have children who were so fond of him. He gave Regan one-third of his kingdom too.

Cordelia, the youngest, was asked to speak last of all. Lear loved his youngest daughter more than either of the others. She knew that her sisters had lied to the old man. They were greedy and dishonest and had tricked their father because he
5 was old and his mind was not clear any more. Cordelia truly loved her father, but she refused to use her love to win his kingdom from him. Besides, her love was so strong that she could not talk about it when she was asked to. She was confident that her father would understand that she could not express her
10 love in words.

When Lear turned to Cordelia and asked her what she would say, she replied, 'Nothing.'

The king was very surprised by her answer. 'If you say nothing, you will get nothing,' he said angrily. Cordelia
15 could only say that she loved her father as much as she ought, and that she could love him no more and no less than that. She did not mean to speak rudely, but Lear was very cross. He told her to be careful or she would not receive her share of the kingdom.

20 'I am your child, and you have cared for me and loved me; I obey you and love you and honour you because of this. But I cannot say, like Goneril and Regan, that I will always love you more than anyone else. If I marry, I will love my husband as much as my father.'

Cordelia finds a good husband

25 King Lear had always had a bad temper, and now that he was old his temper was worse. He was very shocked by what Cordelia said. He did not realize that her words were true and Goneril's and Regan's were false. He told Cordelia that she should no longer call herself his daughter; he would not give
30 her any lands or wealth. The third part of his kingdom, that he had intended to give to Cordelia, he now divided equally between Goneril and Regan. Their husbands, the Dukes of Albany and Cornwall, would rule the kingdom together. Lear decided to keep the title and royal position of a King,

and he decided also to keep one hundred noble soldiers to attend him. He would live with each of his two daughters in turn, staying a month with Goneril and then a month with Regan.

The King's nobles and servants were shocked by his decision, for everyone knew that Cordelia loved him greatly. Only one man dared to speak to the King in her defence. This was the Earl* of Kent, a fair and honest nobleman. When he heard Lear speak angry words to Cordelia, he bravely came forward, and warned the old king that he had rewarded the daughters who loved him least, and punished the one who loved him most. Lear could not control his anger, and told the Earl of Kent to leave the country immediately and for ever. Kent thought he had done his duty by warning Lear, and he accepted this punishment calmly.

Two men had asked the King's permission to marry Cordelia. These were the Duke of Burgundy and the King of France. Lear now called these men to him, and explained that he had punished Cordelia and that she now had no money or possessions. He asked them whether they still wanted to marry her. The Duke of Burgundy did not want to have Cordelia as his wife unless King Lear would give her one-third of the kingdom. Lear refused, and so Burgundy would not marry her. 'I would not marry the Duke of Burgundy anyhow,' said Cordelia, 'because he loves my property, not me.'

The King of France gave Lear a different answer. He admired Cordelia's honesty and courage. 'I cannot believe,' he said to Lear, 'that the daughter you used to love so much can have done anything bad enough to deserve this treatment. If Cordelia will marry me, I will gladly have the daughter Burgundy has refused, and no one will be able to buy her from me.'

'Take her,' said King Lear, 'she is not my daughter now, and I shall never see her face again. Go, Cordelia!'

Crying, Cordelia said good-bye to her sisters. She said she

*Earl, an English nobleman; less important than a Duke.

was not happy about leaving their father with them, but she hoped they would take good care of him. Goneril and Regan answered that she should not try to teach them to do their duty; she should look after her husband, and not worry about them. Cordelia left her father's castle with the King of France, fearing that her sisters would be unkind to the old King.

Goneril is unkind to her father

Cordelia's opinion of her sisters was right, and Lear's was wrong. Soon Goneril and Regan showed their evil intentions. The King said that he would stay with Goneril first, as a guest in her castle. He soon found out how little his eldest daughter loved him, now that he had no power and depended on her kindness. Goneril never tried to make her father welcome in her castle, and she did not want to treat him like a King. She said that he was always complaining and giving orders to everyone, and that his soldiers' behaviour was wild and disorderly. Now that he was only an old man with no kingdom, Goneril had no patience with him. She even told her own servants to treat the King and his followers disrespectfully. They therefore took no notice of Lear's orders, and often pretended they had not heard him. When the old King tried to speak to his daughter about the behaviour of her servants, she made the excuse that she was ill, and refused to see him.

While King Lear was a guest at Goneril's castle, a stranger came to him one day as he was eating dinner. He looked honest and sensible, and the King liked him. The man asked if he could become one of the King's servants. Lear replied, 'Attend me, and if I like you as much after dinner as I do now, I will keep you as one of my servants.'

That evening the stranger had a chance to prove that he was worth something to the King. One of Goneril's servants, who was serving the King's dinner, answered some of the King's questions very rudely. The stranger at once threw the servant out of the room. The King was delighted; he gave the stranger some money and decided to keep him. This stranger was really the Earl of Kent who had been sent abroad by the King. Kent was anxious to serve and defend the old King, and to help him if possible. He had changed his appearance completely, so that he now looked like a servant and could stay near the King. Now that the King was helpless and had begun to act foolishly, Kent thought he needed someone to look after him and protect him from his two evil daughters. When the King asked his name, he said it was Caius.

King Lear still had one other friend, besides Caius. It was usual in those days for Kings to keep amongst their servants men called fools; their duty was to amuse the King with jokes and merry songs, and so to provide him with relief from the serious problems of the state, when he wanted it. A fool was allowed to speak more freely before the King than other people, who had to show great respect for the King's wisdom. Thus a fool had the chance to give serious advice to the King, or to show that he disagreed with his master, if he did it in an amusing way. King Lear had a fool who loved him greatly. This fool tried to cheer him, and stop him from taking his daughter's unkindness too seriously. He used to say, with a laugh, that daughters nowadays wanted obedient fathers, instead of the other way round. He blamed Lear for giving away his kingdom.

Goneril's behaviour towards her father became worse and worse. She decided to make everything so difficult and unpleasant for the King that he would leave the castle. She accused his followers of disorderly behaviour again. Then she said that there were too many of them—Goneril suggested that half as many soldiers would be plenty. It was unnecessary, and expensive for her to keep one hundred men to attend him. Lear was very shocked, and very angry. He did not keep one hundred men to attend him because he needed them, but because they showed that he was still a King and a man who should be respected. When Goneril suggested that he should reduce the number of his men, she showed that she did not intend to think of him as a King any more. Lear cried when he heard his daughter's unkind words, and cursed her for being so cruel and ungrateful. He said he hoped that she would never have a child; if she did have one, he hoped it would make her as unhappy as she had made her father.

Regan punishes Caius

Goneril's husband, Albany, came into the room as they were quarrelling. He tried to calm the King, for he did not
5 approve of Goneril's behaviour. But Lear would not listen to any excuses. He called his servants, and said he would go to stay with his other daughter, Regan, who would be kind to him. But when Lear called for his soldiers he found that, by Goneril's order, fifty of his one hundred men had already been
10 sent away. With his servants and the faithful Caius (the Earl of Kent) he at once left the Duke of Albany's castle.

Just before he started, the King sent Caius with a letter to tell Regan that he was coming. When he reached the Duke of Cornwall's castle, Caius discovered that Goneril had also writ-
15 ten to Regan. She told her sister that she had quarrelled with their father. She warned Regan that he expected his hosts to attend to his needs before anything else; she said that the King would try to bring a large number of followers with him, and she advised Regan not to let them stay. Their father was so
20 bad-tempered, Goneril wrote, that it was impossible to please him.

When they read Goneril's letter, Regan and her husband, the Duke of Cornwall, decided to leave their own castle instead of staying there to welcome the King. They travelled
25 quickly to the castle of the Duke of Gloucester, nearby. Caius followed them there, expecting to get an answer to the King's letter. When he arrived he met the servant of Goneril's who had been so rude to the King at dinner. Caius still hated him for the way he had treated the King. He spoke angrily to him,
30 and offered to fight him. The servant refused to fight, and Caius then attacked and beat him.

At that moment, Regan and her husband arrived; they ordered Caius to be punished for attacking the servant. The Duke of Gloucester, who was with them, said the King would
35 be very annoyed to see his own messenger treated like an

ordinary servant. But Regan and Cornwall did not care, so
Caius was tied up in front of the castle and left there. That was
the first thing the old King saw when he arrived at the Duke
of Gloucester's castle.

This was only the first sign of the way in which Regan would 5
receive him. King Lear asked for his daughter and her
husband; he was told that they were tired because they had
travelled all night, and that they could not see him. When Lear
insisted, Regan and her husband at last came to greet him.
The King told her how unhappy Goneril had made him, but 10
Regan was no kinder than her sister. 'Be patient. I am sure my
sister did her duty towards you. If, as you say, she complained
about your soldiers, I am certain she did it for good reasons;
you should not blame her.' She saw that her father was very
angry, and added, 'You are an old man now, and you should 15
be ruled by others who are wiser than you are. Go back to my
sister and admit that you were wrong.'

Lear could not believe the words he heard. Was Regan sug-
gesting that he, a King, should kneel before his daughter, and
say, 'Dear daughter, I am old and useless now. Please be kind 20
and give me clothes, and food, and somewhere to live?' He
asked Regan, 'How could I do this? And who has tied up my
servant and punished him?'

Lear goes out into the storm

The old King did not believe that Regan meant to be as
unkind to him as Goneril had been. He decided he would stay 25
with her. But just when he was asking about Caius, they heard
people arriving. The King saw that Goneril herself had come
to encourage her sister to be cruel to their father. Regan
welcomed her kindly, and again told Lear to go back and stay
with his eldest daughter. The King would not do this, so Regan 30
told him that she could not possibly have more than twenty-
five of his followers staying in her castle. Even twenty-five,
she said, was too many. He did not need any at all—her own
servants could attend him.

Thus the poor old King stood before his two daughters, and 35 each was unwilling to look after him unless he dismissed all his own servants. Lear had never felt so much sorrow and anger. He cursed them both, and cried that he would take revenge on them for their ungrateful and cruel behaviour. He had given them his kingdom, and they were not even willing to give him somewhere to live! But the two sisters knew that the old man could not really harm them at all—he was helpless.

While Lear wildly cursed and threatened Goneril and Regan, the night became dark and stormy, with thunder, lightning and rain. But still his daughters would not allow Lear's followers to come in. Finally he called for his horses and turned away from the castle. Goneril and Regan saw him, and they let him go. Each told the other that he was an old fool, and that it was his fault, not theirs, that he had no home now. They ordered the Duke of Gloucester to shut the castle doors, and went inside. Outside they had left their old father, half mad with sorrow. They knew there was nowhere for him to shelter—there were not even any trees to keep away the rain. Gloucester did not dare to disobey, but he was very ashamed to shut the King out of his castle.

As the old man went out into the storm his only companion was his faithful fool. Together they wandered around, not knowing where to go. Soon they were both completely wet and very cold. But Lear found his physical suffering less dreadful than the terrible unhappiness in his mind.

In this state the old man was found by Caius, who had escaped at last from the Duke of Gloucester's castle. Caius led them to a broken old hut nearby. The fool went in first, and quickly ran out again crying out that he had seen a ghost. But the ghost was only a poor madman, who called himself 'poor Tom', and talked foolishly. Old Lear assumed that the poor man must have been treated like himself. 'Did you give everything you had to your daughters?' he asked. 'Only unkind daughters could have made you go mad, and left you so poor.' Caius could see that Goneril and Regan had certainly made Lear mad.

Cordelia's love for her father

The next day, the faithful Earl of Kent, or Caius as the King thought he was called, managed, with the help of some friends, to move the King to his own castle. This was on the south coast of England, just across the sea from France. He found men to care for the mad King while he sailed over to France; he went to tell Cordelia, now Queen of France, that her father was in a terrible condition and had been cruelly treated by her sisters. Cordelia, who still loved her father, persuaded her husband, the King of France, to send an army to England to help King Lear. She hoped to defeat and punish Goneril and Regan, and to make her father King of England again. Cordelia herself landed in England with the army.

Meanwhile the King had escaped from the guards Kent had provided to care for him, and was wandering about in the country, singing and talking wildly. He was completely mad. He was discovered by Cordelia's men, but the doctors advised Cordelia not to see her father immediately. They thought that with the help of medicines he would get better, and would then be able to recognize Cordelia. When Cordelia saw the King she was shocked by his appearance. He did not realize who she was at first; he thought someone was trying to trick him because the voice was like Cordelia's voice.

'I am only a foolish old man,' he said, 'and I fear my mind is not perfect now. I can hardly tell where I am, or what I am wearing, or where I slept last night. I think this lady is my child, Cordelia.'

When the old King was sure she was his youngest daughter whom he had sent away without money or lands, he was afraid she would not love him. 'I know you cannot love me; your sisters treated me unfairly, I remember. You have good reasons for not loving me. They had none.'

Cordelia assured him that she loved him still, and had come to help him against his enemies, her sisters. She told him she only wanted to give him peace and rest. Lear felt both great joy and terrible shame. As his memory returned he said to his daughter, 'Forgive and forget; forgive and forget. I am old and foolish.'

When the Dukes of Albany and Cornwall heard about the attack on England by the King of France, they gathered an army and marched quickly against the French forces. Goneril and Regan went with their husbands. The French were beaten, and Lear and Cordelia were captured and made prisoners by Edmund, son of the Earl of Gloucester. Edmund hoped one day to be King of England. He had Cordelia murdered in prison, in the presence of her father. But Lear, in spite of his age and madness, killed the man who was sent to murder her. He could not live long without his dear Cordelia, and he died at her side.

The Earl of Kent, the King's faithful servant, had tried to explain to him that he was the stranger who had become his servant, Caius. But the King could not understand the story, and he never knew how much the faithful Kent had done for him. Kent, an old man, died soon after his master.

Just before King Lear died, he was told what had happened to his other two daughters. Goneril and Regan were as unfaithful to their husbands as they had been to their father. They became enemies of each other, because they both secretly loved the same man—the wicked Edmund, who had captured Lear and Cordelia. Goneril and Regan suspected each other of loving Edmund, but neither was sure. He pretended to each sister that he loved only her. However, when Regan's husband died she told Goneril that she was going to marry Edmund. Soon the two sisters realized that they had each been tricked. Goneril was very angry and jealous, and killed Regan to prevent the marriage. Her own husband, Albany, discovered both her crime and that she had been unfaithful to him. Goneril was put in prison; there she killed herself, in anger and disappointment. Thus the two unkind daughters of Lear died, because of their own wickedness.

Edmund's plan to make himself King failed, for he was killed in a fight with his elder brother. In this way the Duke of Albany, who had not agreed to the murder of Cordelia and had never encouraged his wife's evil treatment of her father, became the new King of Britain.

Questions

The Merchant of Venice

1. Why did Antonio borrow money from Shylock?
2. Why did Shylock hate Antonio?
3. What was the bargain that Shylock offered to Antonio?
4. What was inside the gold, silver and lead boxes?
5. Why did Bassanio choose the lead box?
6. What happened to Antonio's ships?
7. What did Portia ask of Dr. Bellario?
8. Who was the young lawyer?
9. Why did Shylock praise the young lawyer at first?
10. Shylock was not so happy afterwards. What was the reason for this?
11. What was the punishment for a non-Venetian who planned to kill a Venetian citizen?
12. Explain why Shylock was so angry with his daughter, Jessica, and say what he did to make her sorry.
13. What trick did Portia play on her husband?
14. What did Portia accuse Bassanio of doing with the ring she gave him?
15. Why was Bassanio surprised and delighted when Portia showed him Dr. Bellario's letter?

Macbeth

1. How did Duncan reward Macbeth for defeating his enemies?
2. What did the three witches tell Macbeth? Did their words have any effect on him?
3. Describe the feelings of Lady Macbeth after she had read Macbeth's letter.

4. Did Macbeth want to kill Duncan? Give reasons for your answer.
5. Could Macbeth rest after he had killed Duncan? What did he imagine?
6. What did Duncan's two sons decide?
7. Why was Macbeth afraid of Banquo?
8. Describe how Macbeth acted at the feast he gave for the chief nobles.
9. Macbeth wanted to know whether Banquo's children would become Kings of Scotland. What did he see when he asked the witches this question?
10. What did Macbeth's nobles and soldiers do and think after his cruel acts?
11. What strange sight did Macbeth's messenger see?
12. Why was Macduff able to kill Macbeth?

The Tempest

1. How had Caliban come to be Prospero's slave?
2. Describe some of the things Ariel could do which human beings could not.
3. Who was Prospero and how did he and Miranda come to be on the island?
4. How did Prospero test the strength of Ferdinand's love for Miranda?
5. Describe how Ariel made the king and his friends suffer for their evil deeds.
6. What did Alonso and Antonio do when Prospero showed them his real self?
7. What did Prospero do before he left the island?

Hamlet

1. Why was Hamlet unhappy when his mother married again? How did he behave?
2. What did the ghost of Hamlet's father tell Hamlet?
3. What did Hamlet decide to do? Why?
4. Why did Ophelia refuse to see Hamlet?

5. What did the king decide to do with Hamlet?
6. Why did Hamlet ask the actors to perform 'The Murder of Gonzago'?
7. Why did Hamlet not kill Claudius who was praying?
8. Describe how Hamlet killed Polonius.
9. What happened when the sea robbers attacked the ship that Hamlet was on?
10. Whose grave were the workmen digging? How did she die?
11. What did Claudius arrange to make sure that Hamlet would die?
12. Describe what happened at the sword-fighting match.

King Lear

1. What was King Lear's plan in dividing his kingdom into three parts?
2. Why would Cordelia not use her love to win her father's kingdom?
3. What would King Lear do after he had given his kingdom to his daughters?
4. Who was the only person who dared speak in defence of Cordelia? What happened to him?
5. How did Goneril treat King Lear?
6. Who were the King's only two friends?
7. How did Regan treat King Lear?
8. How did the cruel treatment of his daughters affect King Lear? Where did he, his fool and Caius go in the storm?
9. What was Cordelia's plan to help her father?
10. When Cordelia found her father in the country, what were his feelings about her then?
11. In the end, what happened to Goneril and Regan?

Oxford Progressive English Readers

Introductory Grade

Vocabulary restricted to 1400 headwords
Illustrated in full colour

The Call of the Wild and Other Stories	Jack London
Emma	Jane Austen
Jungle Book Stories	Rudyard Kipling
Life Without Katy and Seven Other Stories	O. Henry
Little Women	Louisa M. Alcott
The Lost Umbrella of Kim Chu	Eleanor Estes
Tales from the Arabian Nights	Retold by Rosemary Border
Treasure Island	R.L. Stevenson

Grade 1

Vocabulary restricted to 2100 headwords
Illustrated in full colour

The Adventures of Sherlock Holmes	Sir Arthur Conan Doyle
Alice's Adventures in Wonderland	Lewis Carroll
A Christmas Carol	Charles Dickens
The Dagger and Wings and Other Father Brown Stories	G.K. Chesterton
The Flying Heads and Other Strange Stories	Retold by C. Nancarrow
The Golden Touch and Other Stories	Retold by R. Border
Great Expectations	Charles Dickens
Gulliver's Travels	Jonathan Swift
Hijacked!	J.M. Marks
Jane Eyre	Charlotte Brontë
Lord Jim	Joseph Conrad
Oliver Twist	Charles Dickens
The Stone Junk	Retold by D.H. Howe
Stories of Shakespeare's Plays 1	Retold by N. Kates
Tales from Tolstoy	Retold by R.D. Binfield
The Talking Tree and Other Stories	David McRobbie
The Treasure of the Sierra Madre	B. Traven
True Grit	Charles Portis

Grade 2

Vocabulary restricted to 3100 headwords
Illustrated in colour

The Adventures of Tom Sawyer	Mark Twain
Alice's Adventures through the Looking Glass	Lewis Carroll
Around the World in Eighty Days	Jules Verne
Border Kidnap	J.M. Marks
David Copperfield	Charles Dickens
Five Tales	Oscar Wilde
Fog and Other Stories	Bill Lowe
Further Adventures of Sherlock Holmes	Sir Arthur Conan Doyle

Grade 2 (cont.)

The Hound of the Baskervilles	Sir Arthur Conan Doyle
The Missing Scientist	S.F. Stevens
The Red Badge of Courage	Stephen Crane
Robinson Crusoe	Daniel Defoe
Seven Chinese Stories	T.J. Sheridan
Stories of Shakespeare's Plays 2	Retold by Wyatt & Fullerton
A Tale of Two Cities	Charles Dickens
Tales of Crime and Detection	Retold by G.F. Wear
Two Boxes of Gold and Other Stories	Charles Dickens

Grade 3

Vocabulary restricted to 3 700 headwords
Illustrated in colour

Battle of Wits at Crimson Cliff	Retold by Benjamin Chia
Dr Jekyll and Mr Hyde and Other Stories	R.L. Stevenson
From Russia, with Love	Ian Fleming
The Gifts and Other Stories	O. Henry & Others
The Good Earth	Pearl S. Buck
Journey to the Centre of the Earth	Jules Verne
Kidnapped	R.L. Stevenson
King Solomon's Mines	H. Rider Haggard
Lady Precious Stream	S.I. Hsiung
The Light of Day	Eric Ambler
Moonraker	Ian Fleming
The Moonstone	Wilkie Collins
A Night of Terror and Other Strange Tales	Guy De Maupassant
Seven Stories	H.G. Wells
Stories of Shakespeare's Plays 3	Retold by H.G. Wyatt
Tales of Mystery and Imagination	Edgar Allan Poe
20,000 Leagues Under the Sea	Jules Verne
The War of the Worlds	H.G. Wells
The Woman in White	Wilkie Collins
Wuthering Heights	Emily Brontë
You Only Live Twice	Ian Fleming

Grade 4

Vocabulary within a 5000 headwords range
Illustrated in black and white

The Diamond as Big as the Ritz and Other Stories	F. Scott Fitzgerald
Dragon Seed	Pearl S. Buck
Frankenstein	Mary Shelley
The Mayor of Casterbridge	Thomas Hardy
Pride and Prejudice	Jane Austen
The Stalled Ox and Other Stories	Saki
The Thimble and Other Stories	D.H. Lawrence